EXCELLENCE GUIDE:

Continuous Improvement

Julio Cesar Manella Ribeiro

CONTENTS

EXCELLENCE GUIDE:

AUTHOR:

ENG. JULIO MANELLA

Excellence Guide

CONTINUOUS IMPROVEMENT

2023 EDITION
ENGLIH VERSION

PREFACE:

Welcome to the book "Excellence Guide: Continuous Improvement"!

This book is the result of over two decades of experience in continuous improvement and equipment performance. My journey began as a young Electrical Engineer, freshly graduated from the Barretos School of Engineering, and evolved over years of dedication, learning, and commitment to excellence in my professional career.

Throughout my path in a large multinational company, I had the opportunity to work with equipment maintenance and production lines. It was in this context that I encountered the importance of continuous improvement, the power of identifying waste, and the constant pursuit of innovative solutions. Over 11 years, I immersed myself in equipment performance and continuous improvement, leading projects, implementing tools and methodologies, and achieving significant results.

My passion for sharing knowledge and inspiring other professionals to tread the path of excellence led me to write this book. My goal is to provide you, the reader, with a practical and accessible guide to enhance your knowledge in continuous improvement and equipment performance.

Throughout this book, you will find fundamental concepts of continuous improvement, practical tools, real case studies, and valuable insights based on my professional experience. The practical and action-oriented approach aims to empower you to apply the techniques learned in your own work environment, regardless of your area of expertise.

I believe that continuous improvement is a constant journey, filled with challenges and opportunities for growth. Each step taken towards excellence brings with it the chance to achieve increasingly significant and impactful results.

In this book, I invite you to embark on this journey with me. Each chapter is a door that opens to new perspectives and discoveries. Make the most of this experience, knowing that I am here to support you at every step.

I thank you, dear reader, for joining me on this journey of continuous improvement. I hope this book serves as a valuable guide in your quest for excellence and that you reap the rewards of your own professional development and success.

Happy reading, and may this book be a powerful tool to propel your career and projects towards excellence!

Sincerely,

Eng. Julio Manella

Author of "Excellence Guide: Continuous Improvement"

CHAPTER 1: INTRODUCTION TO CONTINUOUS IMPROVEMENT

Continuous improvement is an essential approach to optimize processes, increase efficiency and productivity, and promote constant enhancement within any organization. In this chapter, we will explore the basic principles of continuous improvement, its historical origin, and its importance in the modern industrial and business contexts.

1.1 What is Continuous Improvement?

Continuous improvement, also known as Kaizen in the Japanese context, is a philosophy and method that aims to gradually improve all aspects of an organization. Its objective is to foster a culture of positive change by encouraging the constant pursuit of improvements in processes, products, services, and, above all, in the development of employees' skills.

The concept of continuous improvement originated in Japan after World War II when Japanese companies, such as Toyota, implemented innovative approaches to overcome challenges and became examples of efficiency and quality. Since then, the idea has spread worldwide and established itself as a fundamental practice to achieve operational excellence.

1.2 The Principles of Continuous Improvement

There are several fundamental principles that underpin continuous improvement. Let's explore the main ones:

1.2.1 Identification And Elimination Of Waste

One of the pillars of continuous improvement is the elimination of waste, known as "Muda" in the Toyota Production System. These wastes can manifest in various forms, such as idle time, excess inventory, rework, among others. By identifying and eliminating them, organizations can increase efficiency and reduce costs, freeing up resources to invest in improvements.

1.2.2 Involvement Of Employees

Continuous improvement relies on the engagement and active participation of all members of the organization. Employees are the foundation of continuous transformation, as they are directly involved in the processes and can provide valuable insights on how to enhance them. Encouraging collaboration and teamwork is crucial for achieving significant results.

1.2.3 Process-Oriented Thinking

Continuous improvement focuses on analyzing and optimizing processes. By understanding and mapping workflow, it is possible to identify bottlenecks and inefficiencies, allowing for effective changes. Process-oriented thinking also involves standardizing best practices, ensuring that acquired knowledge is disseminated and consistently applied.

1.2.4 Pursuit Of Small Incremental Improvements

Continuous improvement values small gradual improvements over major disruptive changes. This gradual approach allows organizations to progress step by step, testing and adapting solutions as needed. By accumulating a series of incremental improvements, long-term results can be remarkable.

1.2.5 Focus On Customer Satisfaction

The customer is at the center of any organization, and continuous improvement aims to meet their needs and expectations. By understanding customer demands and constantly striving to exceed them, companies can strengthen their reputation and build solid relationships with their consumers.

1.3 Methodologies of Continuous Improvement

Over time, various methodologies have been developed to support the practical application of continuous improvement in different contexts. Among the most well-known ones are:

1.3.1 Pdca (Plan-Do-Check-Act)

The PDCA cycle, also known as the Deming Cycle, is an iterative approach that involves four main stages: Plan, Do, Check, and Act. This methodology allows for controlled experiments, where improvements can be tested on a small scale, evaluated, and if successful, implemented gradually.

1.3.2 Dmaic (Define, Measure, Analyze, Improve, Control)

The DMAIC methodology is widely used in the context of Six Sigma, a quantitative approach to continuous improvement. It is based on five stages: Define the problem and improvement objectives, Measure and collect relevant data, Analyze the data to identify root causes, Implement improvements, and Control the results to ensure the sustainability of changes.

1.3.3 5W2h (What, Why, Where, When, Who, How, How Much)

The 5W2H method is a simple and effective tool for planning and executing improvement actions. It involves answering seven key questions: What will be done, Why it will be done, Where it will be done, When it will be done, Who will be responsible, How it will be done, and How much it will cost. This approach helps establish clarity and align efforts towards the improvement objective.

1.4 Tools of Continuous Improvement

In addition to the mentioned methodologies, several tools can be used to support continuous improvement. Some of them include:

1.4.1 Ishikawa Diagram (Fishbone Or Cause And Effect Diagram)

The Ishikawa Diagram is a visual tool that helps identify and analyze possible causes of a problem or improvement opportunity. It organizes causes into major categories, allowing for a structured analysis of factors that may influence a specific outcome.

1.4.2 5 Whys

The 5 Whys method is a technique to identify the root cause of a problem by repeatedly asking "why" a problem occurs. By questioning each answer, it is possible to arrive at the underlying cause and address it effectively.

1.4.3 Pareto Chart

The Pareto Chart is a graphical representation that highlights the relative importance of different elements in a dataset. It follows the principle that most problems are caused by a few key factors. By identifying and prioritizing these factors, efforts can be concentrated where they will have the most impact.

1.4.4 Value Stream Mapping

Value Stream Mapping is a tool used to visualize and analyze the value flow of a process. It shows all the activities involved, from the beginning to the final delivery to the customer. This visualization allows for identifying activities that add value to the process and those that can be considered waste.

1.5 Organizational Culture of Continuous Improvement

A critical aspect for the success of continuous improvement is creating an organizational culture that values and supports it. To achieve this, some practices can be adopted:

1.5.1 Committed Leadership

Leadership plays a crucial role in promoting continuous improvement. Leaders must demonstrate commitment and be role models, encouraging and supporting improvement efforts at all levels of the organization.

1.5.2 Effective Communication

Clear and open communication is essential to involve all employees in the improvement process. It is fundamental to share information about improvement objectives, progress, and results achieved.

1.5.3 Recognition And Rewards

Recognizing and rewarding improvement efforts and results can increase employee motivation and reinforce the culture of continuous improvement. Formal and informal recognitions can be offered to encourage active participation from everyone.

1.5.4 Continuous Learning

Encouraging continuous learning is fundamental to a culture of continuous improvement. Training and development of employees allow them to acquire new skills and knowledge, making them more effective in identifying and implementing improvements.

1.6 Practical Applications of Continuous Improvement

Continuous improvement can be applied in various areas within an organization, resulting in significant benefits:

1.6.1 Improvement Of Production Processes

In the production environment, continuous improvement can lead to reduced cycle times, decreased defects, and better resource utilization. This can result in more efficient production, increased final product quality, and consequently, higher customer satisfaction.

1.6.2 Improvement Of Administrative Processes

In administrative areas, continuous improvement can optimize document management, information flow, and project management. This can streamline internal processes, reduce bureaucracy, and improve decision-making.

1.6.3 Service Improvement

Continuous improvement can be applied in service-oriented sectors such as customer service, technical support, and logistics. By enhancing these services, organizations can strengthen their brand image and increase customer loyalty.

1.6.4 Team Performance Improvement

Continuous improvement can also be used to develop employees' skills and competencies. Training, workshops, and learning opportunities can enhance team performance, driving individual and collective growth.

1.6.5 Innovation And New Product Development

A culture of continuous improvement can stimulate innovation and the development of new products. The constant pursuit of improvements can lead to innovative ideas and creative solutions that meet market needs.

In this first chapter, we have explored the fundamental concepts of continuous improvement, including its definition, principles, methodologies, tools, and practical applications.

Continuous improvement is a dynamic and flexible approach that can be applied in different sectors and organizational contexts.

When properly implemented, it can lead to significant gains in efficiency, quality, customer satisfaction, and competitiveness.

In the next chapter, we will delve into the topic of waste identification and elimination, exploring the main categories of waste and how they can be detected and reduced within an organization.

CHAPTER 2: WASTE IDENTIFICATION AND ELIMINATION

In Chapter 1, we discussed the principles and fundamentals of continuous improvement. Now, let's delve into one of the most crucial aspects of this approach: waste identification and elimination. Waste, also known as "Muda" in the Toyota Production System, refers to activities, processes, or resources that do not add value to the final product or service. Identifying and eliminating these wastes is essential to increase efficiency, reduce costs, and improve process quality.

2.1 The 8 Types of Waste

In the context of continuous improvement, eight main types of waste are recognized. Let's explore each of them:

1. Overproduction: Producing more than needed or before the right time results in excessive inventory, occupies space, and wastes resources.

2. Waiting Time: Occurs when people or machines are idle due to delays, failures, or disorganization in the workflow.

3. Transportation: Unnecessarily moving materials or information between different locations can increase logistics costs and the risk of damage.

4. Overprocessing: Performing additional steps that do not add

value to the product or service, increasing time and resource consumption.

5. Excess Inventory: Maintaining larger inventories than necessary can lead to additional costs, obsolescence, and difficulties in management.

6. Unnecessary Motion: Moving or performing repetitive actions without purpose wastes time and energy.

7. Defects: Products or services with defects require rework or, in severe cases, disposal, leading to financial losses and customer dissatisfaction.

8. Underutilized Skills: Not fully utilizing the potential of employees is a waste of talents and knowledge.

2.2 Waste Identification in Practice

Identifying waste requires a detailed analysis of processes and workflows. Some tools and techniques can assist in this process:

2.2.1 Gemba Walk

The "Gemba Walk" is an essential practice in the philosophy of continuous improvement, especially in the context of Lean Manufacturing and the Toyota Production System. The term "Gemba" is a Japanese word that means "real place" or "where the work happens." The Gemba Walk is an approach where leaders and team members leave their offices or workstations to visit the actual workplace, where operational activities are carried out.

The central idea behind the Gemba Walk is that the best way to understand processes, identify problems, and find opportunities for improvement is by directly observing activities at the place where they occur. By doing so, leaders and team members can gain a holistic view of workflows, interactions with customers and suppliers, working conditions, and production patterns.

Objectives Of The Gemba Walk:

1. Process Understanding: By visiting the workplace, leaders can gain valuable insights into how processes are being executed. They can observe specific steps, cycle times, interactions between employees, and the use of tools and resources.

2. Waste Identification: The Gemba Walk is an opportunity to identify waste and activities that do not add value to the process. By closely observing operations, leaders can identify bottlenecks, excessive inventory, unnecessary movements, and other inefficiencies.

3. Team Engagement: By engaging with the team in the workplace, leaders demonstrate interest in and value the contributions of employees. This increases engagement and motivation for continuous improvement.

4. Problem Resolution: The Gemba Walk is also an opportunity to address challenges in real-time. Leaders can discuss issues with the team, propose solutions, and make immediate decisions for process improvement.

Steps To Conduct A Gemba Walk:

1. Preparation: Before conducting the Gemba Walk, it is essential to define a clear objective. Leaders should have in mind which aspects of the process they want to observe and what problems or improvement opportunities they are seeking.

2. Schedule and Duration: The Gemba Walk should be scheduled at a time when the team is fully active. The duration may vary, but it is important to dedicate enough time to observe processes and

converse with employees.

3. Close Observation: During the Gemba Walk, leaders should pay close attention to workflow and employees, taking note of what they see, listening, and questioning the team when necessary.

4. Dialogue with the Team: The Gemba Walk is not just passive observation but also a dialogue with the team. Leaders should ask questions, obtain insights from employees, and encourage the sharing of improvement ideas.

5. Taking Action: After completing the Gemba Walk, it is essential to take concrete actions based on the observations made. Leaders should discuss the results with the team and implement measures for continuous improvement.

Benefits Of The Gemba Walk:

1. Precise Waste Identification: Being in the workplace allows leaders to identify waste that may not be evident in reports or distant analyses.

2. Creating a Culture of Continuous Improvement: The Gemba Walk demonstrates leadership's commitment to continuous improvement and encourages the team to actively engage in seeking improvements.

3. Quick Problem Resolution: By addressing challenges and issues in real-time, leaders can prevent small problems from becoming significant obstacles.

4. Customer Focus: The Gemba Walk enables leaders to better understand customer needs and expectations, providing a foundation for improving quality and value delivered.

5. Team Engagement: Direct involvement of leaders with the team strengthens the bond between managers and employees,

promoting trust and teamwork.

In summary, the Gemba Walk is a powerful tool for promoting continuous improvement and reinforcing the Lean culture in organizations. By directly observing the workplace, leaders can identify waste, understand processes, engage the team, and take actions to optimize operations and deliver greater value to customers. Practicing the Gemba Walk efficiently involves engaging all levels of the organization in the pursuit of operational excellence.

2.2.2 Value Stream Mapping (Vsm)

Value Stream Mapping is a powerful tool that allows identifying improvement opportunities and waste reduction in processes, helping organizations achieve greater efficiency and effectiveness. We will explore in detail what Value Stream Mapping is, how it is performed, and what the benefits of this practice are.

What Is Value Stream Mapping (Vsm):

Value Stream Mapping, also known as VSM, is a visual tool used to map and analyze the flow of materials and information throughout a process, from the supplier to the final customer. This technique originated in the Toyota Production System and was later adopted in various continuous improvement approaches, such as Lean Manufacturing.

The main objective of Value Stream Mapping is to provide a comprehensive and detailed view of processes, allowing the identification of activities that add value to the product or service, as well as those considered as waste. Based on this analysis, organizations can identify opportunities to optimize the process flow, reduce lead time, eliminate bottlenecks, and increase operational efficiency.

How To Conduct Value Stream Mapping

The Value Stream Mapping (VSM) process involves several steps and requires collaboration from a multidisciplinary team. Let's describe the main steps to conduct VSM:

1. Define the Scope: Start by defining the scope of the mapping. Choose the process that will be mapped and identify the boundaries from the beginning to the end of the value chain. This involves determining which suppliers, activities, and customers will be considered in the mapping.

2. Form the Team: Assemble a team with members from different areas involved in the process. This may include representatives from production, logistics, quality, engineering, among others. The diversity of perspectives contributes to a more comprehensive analysis.

3. Map the Current State: Begin mapping by drawing a detailed flowchart of the current state of the process. Identify all steps, activities, inventory, waiting times, and transportation involved.

4. Identify Waste: With the flowchart of the current state ready, identify the waste present in the process, using the Lean "Seven Wastes" (overproduction, waiting time, transportation, overprocessing, inventory, motion, and defects).

5. Map the Future State: Based on the identified improvement opportunities, work together with the team to design a flowchart of the future state of the process. In this step, the goal is to eliminate or reduce waste and create a more efficient and lean flow.

6. Establish Performance Measures: Determine the key performance indicators (KPIs) that will be used to monitor the

effectiveness of the implemented improvements.

7. Develop an Action Plan: Create an action plan with clear steps to implement the proposed improvements. Define responsibilities and deadlines for each action.

8. Implement Improvements: Put the planned improvements into practice, monitoring and measuring the results obtained.

9. Map the Future Flow: After implementing the improvements, perform a new value stream mapping to verify if the changes brought the desired results and if new improvement opportunities have been identified.

Benefits Of Value Stream Mapping:

Holistic Process View: VSM provides a comprehensive view of processes, enabling the team to understand how activities are connected and how the flow of materials and information occurs.

Identification of Waste: VSM allows for a clear identification of waste present in the process, helping the team prioritize improvement actions.

Elimination of Bottlenecks: Mapping helps identify bottlenecks and choke points, enabling the implementation of actions to improve the process flow.

Team Engagement: VSM involves employees from different areas in a joint analysis of the process, promoting engagement and collaboration among the team.

Reduction of Lead Time: By eliminating waste and optimizing the value stream, organizations can reduce lead time, i.e., the time required to deliver the product or service to the customer.

Value Stream Mapping is a powerful analysis and improvement tool that allows organizations to understand their processes holistically and identify improvement opportunities. By eliminating waste and optimizing the value stream, organizations can achieve greater operational efficiency, cost reduction, and increased customer satisfaction.

It is important to emphasize that Value Stream Mapping is a continuous practice, not a one-time exercise. As organizations evolve and face new challenges, VSM should be updated and reviewed to ensure the ongoing pursuit of operational excellence.

2.2.3 Time And Motion Analysis

Time and motion analysis is a fundamental technique for optimizing process efficiency and productivity by identifying improvement opportunities in task execution. In this chapter, we will explore in detail what time and motion analysis is, how it is conducted, and what the benefits of this practice are.

What Is Time And Motion Analysis:

Time and motion analysis is a technique used to study, measure, and analyze the time required for the execution of each task in a process. The goal is to identify inefficiencies, waste of time and effort, as well as propose improvements to increase productivity and operational efficiency.

This technique was developed in the early 20th century by Frederick Taylor, considered the father of Scientific Management. Through detailed studies, Taylor sought to determine the best method for performing a specific task and establish standard times for its execution.

How To Conduct Time And Motion Analysis:

Time and motion analysis require a systematic and careful approach to obtain accurate results. Let's describe the main steps to conduct this analysis:

1. Select the Task or Process: Start by selecting the task or process to be analyzed. Choose a representative activity, as the results obtained will be applied to similar tasks.

2. Divide the Task into Elements: Divide the task into its individual elements or motions. For example, if the task involves assembling a product, identify distinct steps, such as picking up component A, fitting component B, tightening screws, etc.

3. Record the Time for Each Element: Use an appropriate tool, such as a stopwatch or specific software, to record the time spent on each element of the task. Repeat the process several times to ensure consistent results.

4. Observe Unnecessary Movements: During the analysis, observe unnecessary movements, repetitions, or activities that do not add value to the process. These are indicators of waste and inefficiency.

5. Analyze Results: After collecting the data, analyze the recorded times for each element of the task. Identify bottlenecks, waiting times, and other improvement opportunities.

6. Compare with Theoretical Time: Compare the measured times with the expected theoretical time for the task. The theoretical time is calculated based on reference studies or established standards.

7. Propose Improvements: Based on the analysis, propose improvements to optimize the task execution time. This may involve simplifying processes, training the team, or adopting new technologies.

8. Test and Implement Improvements: Test the proposed improvements on a small scale and assess their impacts. If the results are positive, implement the improvements throughout the

operation.

Benefits Of Time And Motion Analysis:

Identification of Inefficiencies: Time and motion analysis allows identifying activities that consume time and resources unnecessarily, assisting in identifying bottlenecks and waste.

Establishment of Standards: By measuring standard times for tasks, it is possible to establish benchmarks for ideal performance and identify deviations from these standards.

Optimization of Workflow: Based on the analysis results, it is possible to redesign processes to improve the flow of work and reduce the total time required to complete a task or project.

Increased Productivity: By eliminating unnecessary movements and inefficiencies, team productivity and efficiency are enhanced, resulting in increased production capacity.

Data-driven Decision Making: Time and motion analysis provide objective and measurable data that allow for more informed and evidence-based decision making.

Improved Quality: The analysis can also help identify process flaws that may affect the quality of the final product or service, allowing for corrections and improvements.

Time and motion analysis is an essential technique in continuous improvement, allowing organizations to identify inefficiencies, waste, and improvement opportunities in processes. By measuring and analyzing task execution times, companies can optimize workflow, increase productivity, and improve the quality of products or services delivered to customers.

In the next chapter, we will address another important tool used in continuous improvement: the Ishikawa Diagram, also known as the Cause-and-Effect Diagram or Fishbone Diagram. This tool is widely used to identify and analyze root causes of problems and improvement opportunities in processes.

2.2.4 Performance Indicators Review

Performance indicators review is an essential practice to monitor process progress and ensure that the organization's strategic objectives are achieved. Let's explore in detail what performance indicators analysis is, how it is conducted, and what the benefits of this practice are.

What Are Performance Indicators?

Performance Indicators, also known as Key Performance Indicators (KPIs), are quantitative or qualitative metrics that help measure progress towards an organization's strategic objectives. These indicators provide relevant information about process performance and enable the team and leadership to make informed decisions to improve performance.

The Importance Of Performance Indicators Review

The review of performance indicators is crucial to ensure that continuous improvement efforts align with the organization's strategic objectives. Through this practice, the team can monitor progress, identify deviations from goals, and take corrective or proactive actions to enhance performance.

How To Conduct The Performance Indicators Review

The review of performance indicators involves several steps that ensure a comprehensive and effective analysis of the results. Let's look at the key steps to conduct this review:

1. Define Relevant Indicators: Begin by defining performance indicators that are most relevant to the organization's strategic objectives. Ensure that each indicator is measurable, objective, aligned with strategic goals, and has a significant impact on the process or outcome.

2. Collect Data: To conduct the review, it is necessary to regularly collect data related to each performance indicator. This can be done manually or with the support of management systems that automate data collection.

3. Set Goals and Benchmarks: Establish specific goals for each performance indicator based on internal or external benchmarks. These goals should be challenging yet realistic and achievable.

4. Analyze the Results: Perform a detailed analysis of the performance indicator results. Compare the obtained values with the established goals and identify potential deviations.

5. Identify Root Causes of Deviations: If the results are below the set goals, identify the root causes of the deviations. Use tools such as the Ishikawa Diagram or other analysis techniques to identify the main causes of the issues.

6. Take Corrective Actions: Based on the analysis of the results and the causes of deviations, take corrective actions to improve performance. Define a clear action plan, with responsible parties and deadlines for implementing the measures.

7. Monitor Progress: Regularly monitor the progress of the implemented corrective actions and their impact on performance indicators. Keep the team informed about the achieved results and improvements made.

Benefits Of Performance Indicators Review:

Informed Decision Making: The performance indicators review

provides objective and up-to-date information to support decision-making by the team and leadership.

Identification of Improvement Opportunities: Through the analysis of indicators, it is possible to identify opportunities to improve processes, increase efficiency, and the quality of products or services.

Alignment with Strategic Objectives: The review ensures that performance indicators are aligned with the organization's strategic objectives, ensuring that everyone is working towards the same results.

Progress Monitoring: Continuous review of indicators allows tracking progress over time, identifying positive or negative trends that require action.

Focus on Continuous Improvement: By regularly monitoring performance indicators, the organization maintains a constant focus on continuous improvement and striving for better results.

Performance indicators review is an essential practice in continuous improvement, allowing organizations to monitor progress towards strategic objectives and identify improvement opportunities.

By collecting, analyzing, and taking action based on indicators, the team can increase efficiency, productivity, and process quality, ensuring the achievement of desired results.

2.3 Waste Elimination and Improvement Application

After identifying wastes, it's time to develop and implement strategies to eliminate them. Here are some effective approaches:

2.3.1 5S

5S is a practical and efficient approach aimed at creating a more organized, clean, and safe working environment, promoting greater efficiency, productivity, and quality in operations. Let's explore in detail what 5S is, how it is implemented, and what the benefits of this practice are.

What Is 5S?

5S is a Japanese methodology that originated in Japan after World War II, and the five "S"s represent five Japanese words that summarize the fundamental principles of the methodology:

1. Seiri (Sort/Seperate): The first "S" refers to the sorting stage, where the goal is to identify and separate necessary items and materials from those that are unnecessary for the process. This involves eliminating unnecessary items, reducing excess inventory, and creating a more organized work environment.

2. Seiton (Set in Order/Systematize): The second "S" is the stage of setting items in order, where essential items are organized logically and efficiently. Each item should have a designated place, making it easily accessible and reducing wasted time searching for tools or materials.

3. Seiso (Shine/Clean): The third "S" pertains to the cleaning stage. In this phase, a thorough and systematic cleaning of the entire work environment is performed, removing dirt, dust, and waste that may interfere with productivity and work quality.

4. Seiketsu (Standardize): The fourth "S" is the stage of standardization, where standards and procedures are established to maintain the first three "S"s (Sort, Set in Order, and Shine). Standardization ensures that good practices are maintained, and the work environment remains organized and clean over time.

5. Shitsuke (Sustain): The fifth "S" represents the stage of

discipline, where all team members are encouraged to adopt the 5S principles as an essential part of their daily work routine. Discipline is critical to maintaining order and cleanliness over time and ensuring that 5S is effectively implemented and sustained.

How To Implement 5S

The implementation of 5S requires the commitment of the entire team and a systematic approach. Let's describe the key steps to implement 5S:

1. Awareness and Training: Start the implementation process with general awareness of the principles and benefits of 5S. Provide training to the team on how to perform each stage of 5S.

2. Team Formation: Form a team responsible for the implementation of 5S. This team should include members from different areas of the organization to ensure a comprehensive approach.

3. Step by Step: Implement 5S one step at a time, starting with the Sort stage. After completing each stage, move on to the next one. Ensure that each stage is well established before proceeding to the next.

4. Define Responsibilities: Assign clear responsibilities to each team member regarding the maintenance and compliance with 5S principles. Each person should be responsible for their workspace.

5. 5S Audits: Conduct periodic audits to assess the effectiveness of 5S implementation and identify areas that need improvement.

6. Celebrate Results: Recognize and celebrate the efforts and results achieved by the team in each 5S stage. Recognition helps maintain enthusiasm and team commitment.

Benefits Of 5S:

More Organized Work Environment: 5S implementation creates an organized and tidy work environment, where each item has a designated place and is easily accessible.

Increased Productivity: With an organized and clean work environment, the team can perform tasks more efficiently, reducing time spent searching for tools or materials.

Waste Reduction: 5S helps eliminate waste, such as unnecessary inventory, rework, and time wasted searching for items.

Improved Quality: A clean and organized work environment contributes to preventing defects and errors, improving the quality of delivered products and services.

Team Engagement: 5S implementation involves the entire team, contributing to greater engagement and collaboration among members.

5S is a simple yet powerful methodology aimed at creating an organized, clean, and safe work environment, improving the efficiency, and effectiveness of operations.

By implementing the 5S principles, organizations can eliminate waste, improve discipline and focus on continuous improvement, leading to a more efficient and effective work environment.

Continuous practice of 5S is essential to maintaining long-term benefits and promoting a culture of continuous improvement within the organization.

2.3.2 Kanban

Kanban is a visual workflow management tool that originated from the Toyota Production System in Japan. This methodology has become widely adopted in various areas, including software development, project management, customer service, and other activities involving complex workflows. Kanban is known for its simplicity and effectiveness in organizing work, allowing for greater transparency, collaboration, and efficiency. Let's explore in detail what Kanban is, how it works, and what the benefits of this practice are.

What Is Kanban?

Kanban is a Japanese word that means "visual card" or "visual signal." This methodology uses cards (or post-its, magnets, etc.) to represent tasks or work items on a visual board, which is typically divided into columns representing different stages of the workflow. The goal is to create a visual system that allows tracking the workflow clearly and transparently, ensuring that tasks are executed in an orderly and efficient manner.

How Kanban Works

Kanban works through a visual board, which can be physical or digital, and is divided into columns representing different stages of the workflow. Each task or work item is represented by a card that contains relevant information about the task, such as its description, priority, and responsible party. The cards are moved through the columns of the board as they progress through the workflow.

The columns on the board are defined based on the stages of the process, which may vary depending on the nature of the work or the team. For example, a Kanban board for software development may have columns like "To Do," "In Progress," "Waiting for Review," "Testing," and "Done."

Principles Of Kanban:

Kanban is based on some fundamental principles:

1. Work Visualization: The use of a visual board makes work visible to the entire team, facilitating communication, understanding of progress, and identification of bottlenecks.

2. Limit of Work in Progress: Kanban establishes limits for the amount of work that can be in progress in each column. This prevents overloading the team and helps maintain a steady workflow.

3. Flow Management: The focus of Kanban is on managing the flow of work, ensuring that tasks flow quickly and efficiently between the columns of the board.

4. Continuous Feedback: Kanban allows for continuous feedback on process performance, enabling adjustments and improvements over time.

Benefits Of Kanban:

Transparency and Visibility: Kanban provides a clear and transparent view of work in progress, allowing everyone on the team to know what is happening and what the priorities are.

Agility and Flexibility: Kanban is an agile approach that enables quick adaptation to changes, prioritizing tasks according to current needs.

Elimination of Overload: The limit on work in progress avoids team overload, maintaining a sustainable work pace.

Identification of Bottlenecks: Kanban helps identify bottlenecks and issues in the workflow, enabling corrective actions to improve efficiency.

Continuous Improvement: Kanban promotes a culture of

continuous improvement, as teams are constantly seeking ways to optimize workflow and increase productivity.

Kanban is a powerful visual tool that provides efficient and transparent management of workflow. By adopting Kanban, organizations can increase productivity, improve communication and collaboration among teams, and respond quickly to market changes and demands. The simplicity and flexibility of Kanban make it a popular choice for teams seeking to improve their efficiency and achieve more consistent and satisfying results.

2.3.3 Poka-Yoke

Poka-Yoke is a Japanese technique developed by Shigeo Shingo as part of the Toyota Production System, aiming to prevent human errors or defects in processes. The term "Poka-Yoke" can be translated as "error-proofing" or "fail-safe." This approach seeks to create systems or devices that prevent or detect errors before they cause more significant problems. Let's explore in detail what Poka-Yoke is, how it works, and what the benefits of this practice are.

What Is Poka-Yoke?

Poka-Yoke is a philosophy based on the belief that it is better to prevent errors than to correct them. This approach recognizes that humans are prone to making mistakes, and the best way to avoid problems is to design systems or devices that make errors impossible or highly unlikely to occur.

Poka-Yoke devices are designed to be simple and efficient, acting as barriers that prevent errors or as alerts that indicate when an error is about to occur. This technique is widely used in production processes, assembly, and even in daily activities, such as using a key to prevent starting the car with the gear engaged.

How Poka-Yoke Works

Poka-Yoke can be applied in various ways, depending on the specific process or activity. Let's explore some of the most common approaches:

1. Prevention Poka-Yoke: In this approach, devices are designed to prevent an error from occurring. For example, a connector that can only be inserted in a specific position, avoiding incorrect assemblies.

2. Detection Poka-Yoke: In this case, the device is designed to detect an error immediately after it occurs, allowing immediate corrective action. For example, a machine that detects a welding flaw and automatically stops the process.

3. Warning Poka-Yoke: This approach uses visual or auditory signals or alerts to draw attention to a possible failure or error. For example, a light that turns on when a piece is poorly positioned.

4. Sequence Poka-Yoke: In this case, the device is designed to guide the operator in the correct process, ensuring that all steps are followed in the correct order. For example, a checklist to ensure that all steps of a procedure are followed correctly.

Benefits Of Poka-Yoke:

Defect Prevention: The main advantage of Poka-Yoke is the prevention of defects and errors before they occur, resulting in higher-quality products or services.

Cost Reduction: By avoiding the occurrence of defects, Poka-Yoke helps reduce costs associated with rework, repairs, and product returns.

Increased Productivity: By eliminating errors and rework, time and resources can be directed to more productive activities.

Improved Safety: Poka-Yoke can contribute to worker safety by preventing hazardous situations or accidents.

Enhanced Customer Satisfaction: Defect-free products or services lead to greater customer satisfaction, improving the company's reputation.

Poka-Yoke is a valuable approach to continuous improvement, enabling organizations to avoid errors and defects in their processes. By creating fail-safe systems and devices, Poka-Yoke contributes to the production of higher-quality products, cost reduction, and customer satisfaction. It is a simple and effective technique that can be applied in various areas and processes, becoming an essential part of continuous improvement practices in any organization.

2.3.4 Continuous Production Improvement (Kaizen)

Kaizen is a Japanese word that means "change for the better" or "continuous improvement." This management philosophy originated in Japan after World War II, as part of the Toyota Production System. The concept of Kaizen is based on the belief that small continuous and incremental improvements can result in significant gains in efficiency, quality, and productivity over time. Let's explore in detail what Kaizen is, how it is implemented, and what the benefits of this practice are.

What Is Kaizen?

Kaizen is an approach to continuous improvement that involves all members of the organization, from the operational team to top management. This philosophy emphasizes the importance of constantly seeking opportunities for improvement in processes, products, and services, with the aim of achieving higher levels of performance and efficiency.

Kaizen is not limited to technical or technological improvements; it also focuses on behavioral and cultural improvements, encouraging collaboration, creativity, and engagement of all team members.

Principles Of Kaizen:

Kaizen is based on some essential principles:

1. Incremental Improvements: Kaizen advocates small and continuous improvements over time, rather than radical changes. These incremental improvements are easier to implement and are less likely to cause significant disruptions in processes.

2. Involvement of Everyone: Kaizen values the involvement and commitment of all team members, regardless of hierarchical level. Everyone is encouraged to contribute ideas and suggestions for continuous improvement.

3. Elimination of Waste: Kaizen seeks to identify and eliminate waste in processes and activities. Waste is considered anything that does not add value to the final product or service.

4. Customer Focus: The philosophy of Kaizen places the customer as the primary reason for pursuing continuous improvement. Improvements should be directed to meet the needs and expectations of the customer.

How To Implement Kaizen

The implementation of Kaizen requires an organizational culture that values continuous improvement and promotes the active participation of all team members. Some key practices for implementing Kaizen include:

1. Training and Awareness: Provide training for the team

on the principles of Kaizen and the importance of continuous improvement. Create general awareness about the philosophy and benefits of Kaizen.

2. Engage the Team: Encourage and support all team members to actively participate in identifying improvement opportunities. Hold regular meetings to discuss ideas and suggestions.

3. Set Clear Goals: Define clear and specific goals for continuous improvement aligned with the organization's strategic objectives. The goals should be challenging yet achievable.

4. Implement Small and Continuous Improvements: Encourage the implementation of small and continuous improvements in day-to-day operations. Foster a culture of testing new ideas and learning from the results.

5. Track and Measure Progress: Regularly monitor the progress of implemented improvements and measure the achieved results. Use performance indicators to evaluate the effects of the improvements.

Benefits Of Kaizen:

1. Increased Productivity: Continuous improvement leads to more efficient processes, resulting in increased productivity and production capacity.

2. Cost Reduction: Eliminating waste and optimizing processes leads to reduced operational costs.

3. Improved Quality: The constant pursuit of improvement results in higher-quality products and services, increasing customer satisfaction.

4. Team Engagement: Involving the team in the pursuit of improvements promotes engagement and motivation.

5. Agility and Flexibility: Kaizen allows the organization to

adapt quickly to market changes and challenges.

Kaizen is a powerful philosophy of continuous improvement that emphasizes the importance of constantly seeking opportunities for enhancement in processes and practices.

Through incremental improvements, team involvement, and waste elimination, Kaizen enables organizations to achieve higher levels of efficiency, quality, and customer satisfaction.

It is an approach that can be applied in any area of an organization, driving a culture of continuous improvement and the pursuit of excellence in all aspects of work.

Case Study: Application Of Continuous Improvement In A Production Line

In this case study, we will follow the application of the continuous improvement philosophy in a refrigerator assembly line at an appliance factory. The company realized it faced challenges related to efficiency, quality, and customer satisfaction in its refrigerator assembly line. With the aim of improving its processes and achieving better results, the team decided to implement continuous improvement based on Kaizen principles.

Scenario Description:

The refrigerator production line consists of several stations, each responsible for a specific step in the assembly process. The workflow begins with material and parts preparation, followed by chassis assembly, installation of the cooling system, functionality testing, finishing, and final packaging. The company manufactures a wide variety of refrigerator models, making the process complex and demanding.

Identification Of Waste:

After a detailed analysis of the production line, some wastes were identified:

1. Rework and Defects: Before Kaizen implementation, the production line experienced an average rework of 15% due to assembly defects. This resulted in production delays and significant resource wastage.

2. Low Productivity: The average productivity of the production line was 100 refrigerators per day. However, some stations had bottlenecks, limiting the overall production capacity.

3. Material Waste: The company estimated that an average of 8% of materials and parts used in refrigerator assembly were wasted due to mishandling or improper storage.

Elimination Of Waste:

With the identification of waste, the continuous improvement team implemented the following actions:

1. Rework Reduction: The team set a goal to reduce rework to less than 5% within three months.

2. Increased Productivity: The established goal was to increase production line productivity to 120 refrigerators per day, thus meeting market demands.

3. Waste Reduction: The goal was to reduce material waste to less than 5% within six months.

Results Of Continuous Improvement:

After the implementation of continuous improvement, the team achieved the following improvements:

1. Rework Reduction: Rework was reduced to only 3%, well below the set goal of 5%. This resulted in significant cost reduction and improved production line efficiency.

2. Increased Productivity: With the elimination of bottlenecks and standardized work practices, productivity increased to 130 refrigerators per day, exceeding the set goal of 120 refrigerators per day.

3. Waste Reduction: Material waste was reduced to only 4%, achieving the team's goal of less than 5%.

This case study demonstrates that by implementing continuous improvement based on the Kaizen philosophy, significant improvements were achieved in the refrigerator production line. Through problem identification and clear goal-setting, the team reduced rework, increased productivity, and minimized material waste.

These improvements not only led to greater production efficiency and quality but also reinforced the culture of continuous improvement within the company, inspiring the team to constantly seek new enhancement opportunities in all areas of work.

The success of this case study highlights the importance of the Kaizen philosophy as an effective approach to achieving positive and sustainable results in industrial production.

CHAPTER 3: ADVANCED CONTINUOUS IMPROVEMENT METHODOLOGIES

In this chapter, we will explore two of the most recognized and widely used advanced continuous improvement methodologies: DMAIC from Six Sigma and the PDCA cycle. Both methodologies follow a structured and data-driven approach to identify problems, implement changes, and monitor results, aiming to achieve exceptional performance.

3.1 DMAIC: Define, Measure, Analyze, Improve, Control

DMAIC is a widely used methodology in the world of continuous improvement and process management. It represents a cycle of five phases applied to solve complex problems and improve existing processes. The phases of DMAIC are: Define, Measure, Analyze, Improve, and Control.

3.1.1 Define

In this phase, the continuous improvement team clearly defines the problem or improvement opportunity. It is also essential to establish specific and measurable goals aligned with the organization's strategic objectives. The project scope is defined, and relevant stakeholders are identified.

3.1.2 Measure

The measurement phase involves collecting relevant data for the problem at hand. This data is used to understand the current performance of the process and identify gaps between the current state and the established goals. Statistical tools are often used in this phase to analyze the data and gain meaningful insights.

3.1.3 Analyze

In this phase, the collected data is thoroughly analyzed to identify the root causes of the problem. Tools like Ishikawa diagrams and the 5 Whys are employed to delve deeper into the sources of waste and inefficiencies. The continuous improvement team seeks to understand cause-and-effect relationships and identify critical variables for success.

3.1.4 Improve

Based on the analyses conducted, the continuous improvement team develops solutions and carries out experiments to address the identified root causes. It is important to test solutions on a small scale before full implementation to avoid undesirable effects. During this phase, the focus is on effectively implementing improvements.

3.1.5 Control

After the implementation of improvements, it is essential to monitor and control the results to ensure their sustainability. Control mechanisms are established to track performance indicators and ensure that the process remains in line with the established goals. In case of deviations, corrective actions are taken to address them.

3.1.6 Dmaic - Case Study: Reducing Delivery Time In A Food

Delivery Service

We will apply DMAIC in a practical case study to illustrate how this methodology is used.

Phase 1: Define

In this phase, it is important to clearly identify the problem and set the project's goals. In our case study, the food delivery company aims to reduce the average delivery time of orders to improve customer satisfaction and increase service efficiency.

Objectives: Reduce the average delivery time by 20% within a three-month timeframe.

Phase 2: Measure

Here, we will collect relevant data to understand the current performance of the food delivery process. Data will be collected on the delivery time of each order, from the moment the customer places the order until they receive it.

Collected Data:

- Delivery time of each order over the last three months.
- Number of orders delivered on each day of the week.
- Peak and off-peak hours.

Phase 3: Analyze

In this phase, we will analyze the collected data to identify possible causes of the problem and gain a better understanding of the food delivery process. We can use tools such as Pareto charts, scatter plots, and flowcharts to aid in the analysis.

Data Analysis:

- Identification of peak hours with longer delivery times.

- Identification of bottlenecks in the delivery process.

- Analysis of the distribution of delivery times to identify patterns.

Phase 4: Improve

Based on the analyses conducted, we will develop solutions to improve the food delivery process and reduce the average delivery time.

Possible Improvements:

- Reorganize delivery routes to optimize travel and reduce commuting time.

- Allocate more resources during peak hours to expedite deliveries.

- Provide training to delivery personnel to improve delivery efficiency.

Phase 5: Control

In this phase, we will implement the improvements and monitor the results to ensure that the changes have the desired effect and are sustainable over time.

Implementation Of Improvements:

- Reorganization of delivery routes.
- Hiring additional delivery personnel during peak hours.
- Training delivery personnel to optimize the delivery process.

Monitoring And Control:

- Continuous monitoring of delivery times after the

implementation of improvements.

- Comparison of delivery times with the objectives established in the Define phase.

- Conduct periodic assessments to ensure that improvements are maintained.

The application of DMAIC in this practical case study demonstrates how this methodology can be effective in identifying and solving problems, as well as improving existing processes.

Through the DMAIC phases, the food delivery company successfully reduced the average delivery time by 20% within the established timeframe, resulting in a significant improvement in customer satisfaction and operational efficiency.

DMAIC is a powerful tool for achieving concrete and sustainable results in the pursuit of continuous improvement in any business area.

3.2 PDCA Cycle: Plan, Do, Check, Act

The PDCA cycle, also known as the Deming Cycle or Shewhart Cycle, is a continuous improvement cycle widely used to solve problems, improve processes, and achieve better results. It consists of four phases:

3.2.1 Plan

In the planning phase, the continuous improvement team sets clear objectives and identifies the necessary actions to achieve them. Resources and a schedule for implementing the actions are also defined. It is essential to take into account possible lessons learned from previous projects, using available data and information to support decisions whenever possible.

3.2.2 Do

In the execution phase, the planned actions are implemented. At this stage, it is crucial that all involved parties are aware of their responsibilities, and effective communication is established. Processes or changes are put into practice, and data is collected to assess the results.

3.2.3 Check

In this phase, the team verifies the results achieved by comparing them with the objectives set in the planning phase. The collected data is analyzed to evaluate performance and verify if the implemented actions had the expected impact. This involves comparing results before and after the implementation of improvements.

3.2.4 Act

Based on the results analysis, the team makes decisions about what should be done next. If the results were satisfactory, and the objectives were achieved, the team can standardize the changes and implement them on a larger scale. Otherwise, adjustments must be made or other solutions sought to improve performance.

3.2.5 Pdca Cycle - Case Study: Improving The Customer Service Process In A Call Center

We will apply PDCA in a practical case study to illustrate how this methodology is used in practice.

Phase 1: Plan

In this phase, the call center team will plan the actions to improve the customer service process.

1. Problem Identification: The call center has received many customer complaints about the waiting time to speak with an agent and the quality of the received service.

2. Setting Goals: The team establishes clear goals to improve customer service, such as reducing the average waiting time to less than 1 minute and increasing the first-contact resolution rate to 80%.

3. Analysis of the Current Process: The team analyzes the current customer service process, identifying bottlenecks and improvement opportunities.

4. Development of Strategies: Based on the analysis, the team develops strategies to improve the customer service process, such as increasing the number of available agents during peak hours and implementing a triage system to direct customers to the most appropriate agent.

Phase 2: Do

In this phase, the team will carry out the actions planned in the previous phase.

1. Implementation of Strategies: The strategies developed in the planning phase are implemented in the customer service process.

2. Training of Attendants: The attendants are trained in the new practices and procedures to ensure the effectiveness of the implementation.

Phase 3: Check

In this phase, the team will evaluate the results of the actions implemented in the previous phase.

1. Data Collection: The team collects data on the average waiting time, the rate of first-contact problem resolution, and customer feedback after the implementation of the improvements.

2. Analysis of Results: The team analyzes the collected data to verify if the established goals were achieved and if the improvements had the desired effect.

Phase 4: Act

In this phase, based on the analysis of the results, the team will take corrective actions to address any identified issues and consolidate the improvements achieved.

1. Identification of Improvement Opportunities: Based on the analysis of the results, the team identifies additional improvement opportunities to continue enhancing the customer service process.

2. Implementation of Corrective Actions: If any issues are identified, the team implements corrective actions to address those issues.

3. Consolidation of Improvements: The successful improvements are consolidated into the customer service process, becoming integral parts of the working practices.

The application of the PDCA cycle in this practical case study demonstrates how this methodology can be effective in identifying and solving problems, as well as in improving existing processes. Through the PDCA phases, the call center managed to reduce customer waiting time and increase the rate of first-contact problem resolution, resulting in a significant improvement in customer satisfaction and operational efficiency. PDCA is a powerful tool to achieve concrete and sustainable results in the pursuit of continuous improvement in any business area.

3.3 Integration of DMAIC and PDCA

Although DMAIC and the PDCA cycle are distinct methodologies, they can be integrated in a complementary manner. Integrating these approaches can lead to even more robust results:

DMAIC provides a more detailed and data-driven framework for solving complex problems and improving critical processes.

The PDCA cycle is more flexible and can be used to implement smaller changes and quickly assess their impact.

The continuous improvement team can choose the most appropriate approach for each situation, considering the complexity of the problem, the available time frame, and the resources available.

Advanced continuous improvement methodologies such as DMAIC from Six Sigma and the PDCA cycle offer solid frameworks for identifying problems, implementing solutions, and monitoring results. By applying these approaches, organizations can achieve significant improvements in their processes, products, and services, increasing efficiency, reducing costs, and enhancing customer satisfaction. In the next chapter, we will explore how to promote a culture of continuous improvement within the organization, involving and empowering employees at all levels.

CHAPTER 4: CONTINUOUS IMPROVEMENT CULTURE

Successful implementation of continuous improvement requires more than just the application of methodologies and tools. It is crucial to foster an organizational culture that values the constant pursuit of improvement and actively involves all employees in the improvement process. In this chapter, we will explore how to create a culture of continuous improvement and engage members of the organization to become active agents in this process.

4.1 Leadership as an Example

A culture of continuous improvement starts with leadership. Leaders must demonstrate commitment and act as role models by incorporating the principles of continuous improvement into their own practices and decisions. Leadership should provide resources and support for improvement initiatives and acknowledge and reward the efforts of participating employees.

4.2 Clear and Transparent Communication

Effective communication is essential to promote a culture of continuous improvement. Improvement objectives must be clearly communicated to all members of the organization so that everyone understands the purpose of improvement initiatives and their relevance to the company's overall strategy.

Communication should be transparent, open to feedback, and allow employees to freely share their ideas and suggestions.

4.3 Empowerment of Employees

To promote a culture of continuous improvement, it is essential for employees to feel empowered and encouraged to contribute their ideas and perspectives. They should be motivated to identify problems and improvement opportunities in their areas of work and propose creative solutions. Empowering employees increases their sense of ownership and responsibility, leading to greater engagement with improvement initiatives.

4.4 Recognition and Rewards Programs

Recognizing and rewarding improvement efforts and results is a powerful way to encourage a culture of continuous improvement. Formal and informal recognition programs can be established to value employees who excel in their contributions to improvement. This not only motivates employees to continue striving for excellence but also inspires others to follow their example.

4.5 Continuous Learning and Skill Development

A culture of continuous improvement requires a commitment to continuous learning and skill development. Employees should be encouraged to seek opportunities for training and development that help them acquire new knowledge and skills relevant to continuous improvement. This includes not only technical training but also leadership, critical thinking, and problem-solving skill development.

4.6 Encouragement of Innovation and Experimentation

A culture of continuous improvement should encourage innovation and experimentation. Employees should feel comfortable proposing new and creative ideas, even if some of them may not work. Errors and failures should be seen as learning opportunities, not reasons for punishment. By encouraging innovation, the organization can discover innovative solutions that drive continuous improvement significantly.

4.7 Sharing Best Practices and Success

Sharing best practices and success stories is a powerful way to reinforce the culture of continuous improvement. Sharing positive results and recognizing teams and individuals who achieved significant improvements inspire other employees to engage in the improvement process. Knowledge sharing also helps create a collaborative environment where employees can learn from each other and support one another.

4.8 Continuous Monitoring and Evaluation

A culture of continuous improvement must be constantly monitored and evaluated to ensure that initiatives are generating the expected results. Leaders should track performance indicators and the progress of improvement initiatives and conduct regular reviews to identify opportunities for enhancement. Feedback from employees is also essential in this process, allowing them to express their opinions and suggestions to improve the culture of continuous improvement.

4.9 Example of Implementing a Continuous Improvement Culture

Let's explore a practical example of how a company implemented a culture of continuous improvement:

Leadership Commitment

The top management defined continuous improvement as a strategic priority and demonstrated their commitment to this approach.

Transparent Communication

Leaders communicated the vision of continuous improvement to all employees, explaining objectives and the significance of this culture for the organization's success.

Employee Empowerment

Employees were encouraged to identify problems and improvement opportunities in their areas, and their ideas were valued and considered in decision-making.

Recognition Programs

The company implemented recognition programs to value employees who excelled in their contributions to continuous improvement, fostering a healthy competitive environment.

Skill Development

Opportunities for training and development were provided to

employees, covering technical skills, leadership, and problem-solving abilities.

Innovation Encouragement

The company encouraged innovation, motivating employees to propose new ideas and experiment with creative solutions.

Sharing Best Practices

Teams shared best practices and success stories in regular meetings, inspiring other employees to engage in continuous improvement.

Continuous Monitoring

A monitoring and evaluation system was established to track the progress of improvement initiatives and make necessary adjustments.

A culture of continuous improvement is a key element for the success of improvement initiatives in any organization.

By promoting exemplary leadership, transparent communication, employee empowerment, and recognition of results, it is possible to create an environment conducive to innovation and the constant pursuit of excellence.

In the next chapter, we will explore how continuous improvement can be applied in different sectors and types of businesses, presenting practical success examples in various areas of industry and services.

CHAPTER 5: APPLICATION OF CONTINUOUS IMPROVEMENT IN DIFFERENT SECTORS AND BUSINESSES

Continuous improvement is a highly versatile and effective approach that can be applied in various sectors and types of businesses. In this chapter, we will explore practical cases of companies and organizations that have successfully adopted continuous improvement in different contexts. We will analyze how this approach has provided significant benefits, driven operational efficiency, increased customer satisfaction, and contributed to the competitiveness and success of organizations.

5.1 Manufacturing Sector

The manufacturing sector is one of the primary beneficiaries of continuous improvement. Through this approach, companies can optimize production processes, eliminate waste, reduce costs, and improve product quality. Let's explore a case study of an automotive company that successfully implemented continuous improvement in its production line.

Case Study: Automotive Company "Excelcar"

The automotive company "ExcelCar" is known for its constant pursuit of excellence and innovation in the automotive industry. Faced with increasing demand for vehicles and fierce competition in the market, the company realized the need to enhance its production line to meet customer expectations and maintain its competitive position.

To identify and eliminate inefficiencies, the continuous improvement team at "ExcelCar" chose to use Value Stream Mapping (VSM). This tool allows them to map the entire production process, from the receipt of raw materials to the delivery of the finished vehicle to customers. During this process, the team identified bottlenecks in the production flow, excessive waiting times between stages, and unnecessary operations.

Based on the VSM analysis, the company applied the DMAIC methodology of Six Sigma to address the identified problems and implement significant improvements. The DMAIC phases were applied as follows:

1. Define: In this phase, the team clearly defined the project's objective, setting specific goals to reduce the total production time and improve the quality of the final product. They also identified the key stakeholders involved in the production process and their needs.

2. Measure: The team collected detailed data on the time spent at each production stage, identifying bottlenecks and areas that demanded the most time and resources. An analysis of defects and rework in finished vehicles was also performed.

3. Analyze: The collected data was thoroughly analyzed to identify the root causes of the problems, including prolonged setup times, delays in parts delivery, and communication failures between teams. The team held meetings with operators,

engineers, and managers to understand their perspectives and gather additional information.

4. Improve: Based on the analysis, the team developed and implemented solutions to address the root causes of the problems. The improvements included optimizing the production sequence, reducing setup times through standardization, and adopting a more flexible and adaptable production line.

5. Control: To ensure the sustainability of the improvements, the team established control and monitoring systems to track key performance indicators and ensure that the enhanced processes were maintained over time. Quality standards were also established to verify the compliance of finished products.

With the implementation of these improvements, "ExcelCar" achieved impressive results. The total production time was reduced by 30%, resulting in greater production line efficiency and an increased capacity to meet customer demands promptly. Additionally, the quality of vehicles significantly improved, with a 50% reduction in the number of defects reported by customers.

The company also reaped other indirect benefits, such as a more collaborative work environment, engaged employees who were satisfied with the achieved results, and a stronger market reputation for delivering high-quality products with reliable delivery times.

5.2 Service Sector

The service sector also significantly benefits from continuous improvement. In this context, the approach is essential to ensure excellence in customer service, optimize processes, and increase customer satisfaction. Let's explore a case study of a customer service company that successfully implemented continuous improvement to enhance service efficiency and quality.

Case Study: Customer Service Company "Servicenow"

"ServiceNow" is a customer service company that provides technical support and assistance to customers from various businesses. With a high volume of daily calls and the need to provide quick and accurate responses to customers, "ServiceNow" faced challenges in maintaining service efficiency and customer satisfaction.

To improve service quality and reduce customer waiting time, the continuous improvement team at "ServiceNow" decided to apply the PDCA cycle to make incremental and continuous improvements to the service process.

1. Plan: The team identified the main issues faced in customer service, such as long waiting times, lack of standardization in procedures, and low customer satisfaction. They established specific goals to reduce the average waiting time and improve service quality.

2. Do: Based on the planning, the team implemented changes in the service procedures, developed standardized scripts to guide the attendants, and adopted more efficient technical support tools.

3. Check: After implementing the improvements, the team monitored the results, collecting data on the average waiting time, customer satisfaction, and problem resolution in calls.

4. Act: Based on the analysis of the results, the team identified that the average waiting time was reduced by 40%, and customer satisfaction increased by 25%. However, they noted that there was still room for additional improvements in resolving more

complex issues.

5. Replan: The team decided to revise the service scripts and implement new training focused on empathy and resolving more complex issues. Additionally, they established a continuous customer feedback system to ensure their needs were addressed more effectively.

With these improvements, "ServiceNow" achieved remarkable results. The average waiting time was halved, resulting in higher customer satisfaction and retention of more satisfied customers. The company also experienced a significant increase in operational efficiency, with a better-trained service team aligned with standardized procedures.

Moreover, the implementation of a culture of continuous improvement at "ServiceNow" led to increased employee motivation, as they felt valued for their contributions to the improvements. This resulted in reduced employee turnover and a more productive and collaborative work environment.

5.3 Healthcare Sector

The healthcare sector also greatly benefits from continuous improvement. In this context, the approach is crucial to enhance the quality of care, reduce medical errors, and optimize hospital processes. Let's explore a case study of a regional hospital that applied continuous improvement to improve patient safety and operational efficiency.

Case Study: Regional Hospital "Lifecare"

The regional hospital "LifeCare" is an institution that constantly strives for excellence in medical care and patient safety. Faced with challenges such as high rates of hospital-acquired infections and waste management issues, the "LifeCare" continuous improvement team decided to implement the DMAIC approach to address these issues.

1. Define: The team defined the project's goal as reducing hospital-acquired infection rates and improving waste management. They set clear goals to decrease infection incidence and implement a more efficient system for hospital waste management.

2. Measure: To identify the severity of the problem, the team collected data on the number of hospital-acquired infections recorded over a specific period and assessed the current waste management system.

3. Analyze: Data analysis revealed that most infections were related to inadequate hand hygiene and failures in waste management, leading to the spread of bacteria and viruses.

4. Improve: The team implemented a series of changes, including training for the medical and nursing staff on the importance of hand hygiene, installing alcohol gel dispensers in strategic locations, and adopting rigorous procedures for hospital waste management.

5. Control: To ensure the sustainability of the improvements, control and monitoring systems were established to track the number of hospital-acquired infections and the effectiveness of the implemented measures.

With the implementation of these improvements, "LifeCare" achieved remarkable results. The number of hospital-acquired infections was reduced by 50%, resulting in a significant improvement in patient safety and the quality of care provided.

Furthermore, the adoption of a more efficient hospital waste management system led to a significant reduction in contamination risks and infection spread. These improvements contributed to "LifeCare's" solid reputation as a hospital that prioritizes patient safety and well-being.

5.4 Technology Sector

The technology sector also greatly benefits from continuous improvement. In this context, the approach is essential to ensure the quality of products and services offered and to drive continuous innovation. Let's explore a case study of a software development company that successfully implemented continuous improvement in their development processes.

Case Study: Software Development Company "Techsoft"

"TechSoft" is a software development company that continuously strives for excellence in its products and services. With a growing demand for innovative and high-quality solutions, "TechSoft" recognized the importance of continuous improvement in its development processes.

To enhance the efficiency and quality of its products, the "TechSoft" continuous improvement team decided to apply the PDCA cycle, aiming to make incremental and continuous improvements in the development process.

1. Plan: The team identified the main problems faced in the development process, such as lack of communication between teams and difficulty meeting tight deadlines.

2. Do: Based on the planning, the team implemented changes in

team communication, introducing daily meetings to align project progress and expectations for the day.

3. Check: The team monitored the results after implementing the improvements, collecting data on the effectiveness of daily meetings and the ability to meet deadlines.

4. Act: Based on the analysis of the results, the team realized that daily meetings were improving communication and collaboration between teams, but there was still a need to improve the definition of more realistic deadlines.

5. Replan: The team decided to review the deadline-setting processes, involving the teams in estimating time for each project stage and adopting a more realistic schedule.

With these improvements, "TechSoft" achieved remarkable results. Communication between teams was enhanced, resulting in more efficient alignment and reduced rework. Moreover, the definition of more realistic deadlines led to increased customer satisfaction as the company could deliver projects within the agreed-upon timeframe.

These improvements allowed "TechSoft" to stand out in the market as a company that offers high-quality software solutions, delivered in an agile manner and within established deadlines. Continuous improvement has become an essential part of the company's culture, constantly seeking ways to enhance its processes and products to meet customer needs and expectations.

5.5 Educational Sector

The educational sector can also benefit immensely from continuous improvement. In this context, the approach is crucial to ensure the quality of education, increase student retention, and improve academic performance. Let's explore a case study of a university that successfully implemented continuous improvement to enhance its academic and administrative processes.

Case Study: "EducaMais" University

"EducaMais" University is known for its commitment to excellence in higher education and student satisfaction. With the goal of improving its academic and administrative efficiency, the "EducaMais" continuous improvement team decided to apply the DMAIC methodology to address identified challenges.

1. Define: The team defined the project's goal as improving academic and administrative processes, focusing on reducing student enrollment response time and the efficiency of the student performance evaluation process.

2. Measure: The team collected detailed data on the time spent in each enrollment step and the time required to complete the student performance evaluation process.

3. Analyze: Data analysis revealed that the average enrollment response time was above expectations due to a lack of standardization in procedures, while the student performance evaluation process suffered from overload on evaluators.

4. Improve: The team implemented changes in the enrollment process, establishing clear deadlines and standardized procedures to streamline the process. Additionally, online performance evaluation tools were adopted to facilitate the evaluation process.

5. Control: The team established control and monitoring systems to track enrollment response time and the effectiveness of the changes implemented in the performance evaluation

process.

With these improvements, "EducaMais" University achieved impressive results. The average enrollment response time was reduced by 50%, allowing students more time to prepare for the start of the semester. Additionally, the performance evaluation process became more efficient, providing a more detailed analysis of student performance and identifying opportunities for academic improvement.

These improvements contributed to higher student satisfaction and retention, as students felt more supported and engaged in the university's academic processes. The implementation of a continuous improvement culture at "EducaMais" also led to increased employee engagement, as they felt valued for their contributions to the improvements and, as a result, became more committed to the university's success.

As seen in the case studies, continuous improvement is a highly effective approach for enhancing processes, optimizing operations, and achieving exceptional results in various sectors and types of businesses. The case studies presented in this chapter illustrate how companies and organizations from different industries successfully implemented continuous improvement and reaped significant benefits.

Through Value Stream Mapping, DMAIC, the PDCA cycle, and other methodologies, companies can identify improvement opportunities, eliminate waste, and enhance the quality of products and services. Additionally, by promoting a culture of continuous improvement, organizations can foster employee engagement, teamwork, and innovation, making them more competitive and successful in an ever-evolving market.

In the next chapter, we will conclude the book by providing additional guidance for implementing continuous improvement and sharing final insights on the importance of this approach for the ongoing success and growth of organizations.

CHAPTER 6: IMPLEMENTING CONTINUOUS IMPROVEMENT - GUIDELINES AND INSIGHTS

In this final chapter, we will explore practical guidelines for the successful implementation of continuous improvement in organizations, as well as valuable insights to maximize the benefits of this approach. Continuous improvement is an ongoing journey, and it is essential to establish a culture of learning, adaptation, and constant enhancement to achieve lasting results.

6.1 Establishing a Culture of Continuous Improvement

To effectively implement continuous improvement in an organization, it is crucial to establish a culture that fosters a constant pursuit of enhancement. Here are some guidelines to promote this culture:

1. Leadership Commitment: The support and commitment of top leadership are crucial to the success of continuous improvement. Leaders should demonstrate the value of this approach, actively engage in improvement projects, and provide the necessary resources for successful initiatives.

2. Involvement of Employees: Continuous improvement cannot be solely a leadership initiative; it requires the participation and engagement of all employees. Encourage collaboration, exchange

of ideas, and participation in improvement projects, creating an environment where employees feel empowered and encouraged to contribute.

3. Transparent Communication: Maintain open and transparent communication regarding continuous improvement initiatives. Keep employees informed about objectives, results, and next steps of ongoing initiatives. This will help maintain enthusiasm and interest among all involved parties.

4. Recognition and Celebration: Recognize and celebrate achievements attained through continuous improvement. Show gratitude and acknowledge employees who contributed to the success of improvement projects. This appreciation will reinforce the culture of continuous improvement and encourage the pursuit of new enhancement opportunities.

5. Learning and Development: Promote a culture of continuous learning, where employees are encouraged to seek new knowledge and skills. Provide training in tools and methodologies for continuous improvement, enabling everyone to contribute to the projects effectively.

6.2 Defining Priorities and Selecting Projects

An organization may have various areas and processes that can benefit from continuous improvement. However, it is essential to define priorities and select the most relevant projects for the company's strategy. Here are some steps to guide the project selection process:

1. Alignment with Strategy: Analyze the overall strategy of the organization and identify which areas or processes align with

strategic objectives. Prioritize projects that have a greater impact on achieving strategic goals and priorities.

2. Identification of Opportunities: Conduct a detailed analysis of existing processes to identify improvement opportunities. These opportunities may be found through customer feedback, performance indicators, complaints, or identified bottlenecks.

3. Feasibility and Resources: Evaluate the feasibility of each project in terms of human, financial, and technological resources required. Ensure that the organization has the capacity to implement the proposed improvements effectively.

4. Expected Benefits: Estimate the expected benefits of each project, both in terms of quantitative results, such as cost reduction or revenue increase, and qualitative benefits, such as improved customer satisfaction or work environment.

5. Prioritization and Selection: Rank the projects based on strategic importance, expected impact, and feasibility. Select the most relevant projects to initiate and develop a timeline for implementation.

6.3 Tools and Methodologies of Continuous Improvement

There are several tools and methodologies that can be used to implement continuous improvement. Some of the most popular ones include:

1. Value Stream Mapping (VSM): This tool visualizes the entire value stream of a process, identifying improvement opportunities, and eliminating waste.

2. DMAIC: This Six Sigma approach is a structured methodology with five steps - Define, Measure, Analyze, Improve, and

Control - to address complex problems and achieve sustainable improvements.

3. PDCA Cycle: The PDCA cycle - Plan, Do, Check, Act - is a management methodology aimed at continuously improving processes through cyclic stages of planning, execution, verification, and corrective action.

4. Kaizen: The Japanese concept of Kaizen refers to the continuous pursuit of incremental improvements in all aspects of the organization, involving all employees in improvement initiatives.

5. 5 Whys: A simple yet powerful technique to identify the root cause of a problem, asking successive "why" questions until reaching the origin of the issue.

The choice of tools and methodologies to be used will depend on the nature of the project and the specific needs of the organization. The important thing is to select the most suitable tools to address specific challenges and achieve the desired results.

6.4 Monitoring and Measuring Results

A critical aspect of continuous improvement is the ongoing monitoring and measurement of results. It is essential to track the progress of improvement projects and evaluate the impact of the implemented changes. Here are some guidelines for effective monitoring:

1. Establish Key Performance Indicators: Define key performance indicators (KPIs) that are relevant to the ongoing improvement projects. These indicators will enable measuring

progress and evaluating whether the results align with established objectives.

2. Data Collection: Ensure systematic and accurate data collection relevant to each improvement project. Utilize tools and information systems to facilitate data collection and analysis.

3. Result Analysis: Regularly conduct analyses of the outcomes achieved through improvement initiatives. Identify successes, lessons learned, and areas that still require attention.

4. Customer and Employee Feedback: Listen attentively to customer and employee feedback regarding the implemented improvements. This feedback will provide valuable insights into the effectiveness of the changes and opportunities for continuous enhancement.

5. Corrective Actions: Based on result analysis, implement corrective actions when necessary. If the outcomes do not align with established goals, identify root causes and adjust improvement strategies accordingly.

Sure, here's the translation:

6.5 Fostering Innovation and Creativity

Continuous improvement and innovation are inherently interconnected. To drive continuous improvement, it is essential to foster a culture of innovation and creativity within the organization. Here are some strategies to encourage innovation:

1. Idea Spaces: Create spaces and opportunities for employees to share ideas and suggestions to enhance processes, products, and

services.

2. Diversity and Inclusion: Value diversity and inclusion, as diverse perspectives bring new ideas and innovative solutions.

3. Controlled Experimentation: Encourage experimentation with new approaches, but in a controlled manner with evaluation of results.

4. Recognition of Innovation: Recognize and reward innovative ideas and initiatives to motivate employees to contribute creative suggestions.

5. External Partnerships: Establish partnerships with other organizations, universities, or research centers to seek inspiration and external knowledge.

6.6 Dealing with Challenges and Resistance

Implementing continuous improvement may face challenges and resistance at various stages. It is important to be prepared to address these obstacles and overcome them. Here are some guidelines to tackle challenges:

1. Education and Training: Provide training on the continuous improvement approach and its methodologies to the entire team, so everyone understands the benefits and processes involved.

2. Effective Communication: Clearly communicate the objectives and benefits of continuous improvement to the entire team and involve employees in the decision-making process.

3. Change Management: Identify and address resistance and concerns through effective change management, highlighting the benefits for the team and the organization.

4. Celebration of Achievements: Recognize and celebrate

successes achieved during the continuous improvement process to maintain enthusiasm and motivation among the team.

5. Learning from Failures: Accept that not all improvement projects will be successful. Learn from failures and use them as opportunities for improvement.

6.7 Sustainability of Continuous Improvement

For continuous improvement to be sustainable, it must become an integral part of the organizational culture. Here are some strategies to ensure the continuity of continuous improvement:

1. Continuous Leadership: The leadership must continue to support and promote the culture of continuous improvement, reinforcing its importance throughout the organization.

2. Training and Development: Invest in continuous training and development so that employees can stay updated with the tools and methodologies of continuous improvement.

3. Feedback and Evaluation: Establish a system of continuous feedback to evaluate results and identify new opportunities for improvement.

4. Recognition and Reward: Continue to recognize and reward employees' contributions to improvement initiatives, fostering a culture of learning and innovation.

5. Knowledge Sharing: Encourage knowledge and best practice sharing among teams, so everyone can benefit from lessons learned.

6. Resilience Culture: Promote a culture of resilience, where employees are encouraged to learn from challenges and adapt to changes quickly.

Conclusion

Continuous improvement is a powerful approach to enhance processes, optimize operations, and achieve exceptional results in organizations of all sectors and sizes. In this book, we explored the fundamental concepts of continuous improvement, from its origins to its applications in various contexts.

By implementing continuous improvement, organizations can boost efficiency, reduce costs, improve the quality of products and services, increase customer satisfaction, and drive continuous innovation. However, it is important to remember that continuous improvement is an ongoing journey that requires commitment, patience, and perseverance.

By establishing a culture of continuous improvement, selecting relevant projects, using appropriate tools and methodologies, monitoring results, and fostering innovation, organizations will be on the right path to long-term success.

Continuous improvement is more than just a methodology; it is a mindset that promotes the constant pursuit of improvement, learning, and adaptation. By adopting this approach, organizations will be prepared to face the challenges and opportunities of the future, becoming more competitive, resilient, and successful in an ever-evolving business landscape.

CHAPTER 7: BONUS

Access Link to Templates and Satisfaction Survey

For reference, use the link or the QR code to access a folder on Google Drive. I recommend downloading the files to your computer before use and modify them as you see fit. Happy using!

Access the link or use your phone to scan the QR Code.

Templates - Google Drive	Survey
Templates	Survey